A gift for

_____

From

_____

Date

_____

GOD'S STRENGTH  FOR HARD TIMES

BILLY GRAHAM

THOMAS NELSON
Since 1798

ISBN 978-1-4002-4423-2 (HC)
ISBN 978-1-4002-4429-4 (audiobook)
ISBN 978-1-4002-4428-7 (eBook)

Printed in Malaysia

24 25 26 27 28 OFF 10 9 8 7 6 5 4 3 2 1

CONTENTS

FOREWORD

Storm clouds continue to gather heavily around the world, even darkening our own doorsteps. News headlines scream with anguish and heartache. At the time of this writing, I had just returned from Israel days after it was viciously attacked by terrorists on October 7, 2023. Over 1,200 people were killed and 240 taken hostage. I had visited several *kibbutzim* (communal settlements) and saw homes that had been burned and scarred, with craters in the floors and shrapnel pieces embedded in the walls. I witnessed bitterness and anguish like I've never seen before. It seemed like every demon of hell had been loosed.

International conflict has defined Israel's history. The Jewish people of this small but important nation have endured captivity and exile from a succession of hostile world powers. Still today we watch evil perpetrated against God's people. This is nothing new.

In the book of 1 Samuel, we read about a woman named Hannah, despondent that she could not give her husband a son. She went to the temple and "in bitterness of soul . . . prayed to the LORD and wept in anguish," asking Him to look upon her affliction (1:10 NKJV).

"Bitterness of soul" is prevalent around the world. And God has not forgotten us. There are people in our own families and neighborhoods who are overcome with untold anguish. Suffering can cause us to doubt God's mercy and love, but the devil is defeated when we fix our eyes on God and trust in Him. If you have forgotten God, repent and turn to Him for salvation.

My father preached about human emotion that batters the mind. He wrote of the utter despair that can bring us to our knees: "Life has its share of joys and laughter—but we also know life's road is often very rough. Temptations assail us; people disappoint us; illness and age weaken us; tragedies and sorrows ambush us; evil and injustice overpower us. As long as we look only at circumstances," he said, "life will be very hard, but when we depend upon His strength and guidance, God will bring peace in the midst of the storms."

Perhaps you are in bitterness of soul, seeking God for answers to life's problems. We don't need to look to technology or politics or the Iron Dome for refuge. God's Word is our fortress. His truth touches hearts and shows that by the power of His strength in hard times, men and women can be overcomers while on the journey called life. This is God's promise.

We find this hope throughout the book of Psalms, written during the reigns of King David and his son King Solomon. When we focus our minds on Almighty God, He will comfort our troubled hearts, and we can say by His power, "The LORD is my rock and my fortress and my deliverer; my God, my strength, in whom I will trust; my shield and the horn of my salvation, my stronghold" (Psalm 18:2 NKJV).

—FRANKLIN GRAHAM
Boone, North Carolina
January 2024

One

GOD STRENGTHENS
FAITH IN HARD TIMES

As you received Christ Jesus

the Lord, so walk in him,

rooted and built up in him

and established in the faith.

COLOSSIANS 2:6–7 ESV

_____

It is no accident that the Bible compares us to trees, urging us to be sure our spiritual roots are deep and strong. The psalmist wrote that the godly person "is like a tree planted by streams of water, which yields its fruit in season" (Psalm 1:3). But a tree wasn't always a tree. It began as a small seed, which in time sprouted and became a seedling. If conditions were right, that fragile seedling grew into a sapling and finally into a mature tree.

The same is true of spiritual life. It begins with the seed of God's Word planted in the soil of our souls that eventually sprouts and becomes a new seedling. But—like a tree—that spiritual seedling isn't intended to remain a seedling forever. It is meant to grow and become strong and mature, bearing fruit that is pleasing to God.

The Bible illustrates this truth in another way. When we come to Christ, the Bible says, we are like newborn babies—bursting with life but helpless and weak and vulnerable to every kind of danger. But a baby isn't meant to remain that way forever. Infants are meant to grow and eventually become adults—no longer helpless, weak and vulnerable; able to take care of themselves and have full and productive lives.

The same is true for us spiritually. When we come to Christ, we are born again—that is, God our heavenly Father works in our hearts by His Holy Spirit to give us new life as His children (John 3:1–17). But we aren't meant to remain spiritual infants. God's will is for us to grow strong in our faith and become spiritually mature, grounded in the truth of His Word and firmly committed to doing His will.

What is spiritual maturity? To put it another way, what does God want to do in your life?

The Bible's answer can be put into one sentence: *God's will is for us to become more and more like the Lord Jesus Christ.* He wants to change us from within, taking away everything that dishonors Him and replacing it with Christ's love and purity. From all eternity, God's plan was that we would be "conformed to the image of his Son, that he might be the firstborn among many brothers and sisters" (Romans 8:29). This is spiritual maturity: to become more and more like Christ in our "love, joy, peace, patience, kindness, goodness, faithfulness, gentleness, and self-control" (Galatians 5:22–23 NLT).

Will we ever reach this goal? No, not completely in this life—but someday we will enter God's presence forever, and then we will be totally free from sin's grip.

So does this mean it is hopeless to strive for spiritual maturity in the present?

We aren't meant to remain spiritual infants. God's will is for us to grow strong in our faith and become spiritually mature.

No! God wants to begin changing us from within and making us more like Christ right now. In heaven that process will be complete; sin's power over us will be destroyed, and we will inherit that heavenly home Christ has prepared for us.

The key is this: God wants us to be spiritually strong and has provided us with every resource we need. In ourselves we are weak, so if we try to meet life's struggles and temptations on our own, we fail. We need God's strength to face life's challenges. He will strengthen us in faith as we learn to trust Him. As Peter reminded us, "His divine power has given us everything we need for a godly life through our knowledge of him who called us by his own glory and goodness" (2 Peter 1:3).

A friend of mine and his wife began researching where they might retire. A prerequisite was finding a place where he could have a woodworking shop.

"What is your favorite wood to work with?" I asked him one day.

"I suppose it would be from the trees that grow along the ridgetops of the Appalachian Mountains," he answered.

"Why?"

"Because of the harsh climate, those trees grow very slowly," he replied. "As a result the wood is tough and close-grained, which makes it hard to carve; but anything made from it will be durable and very beautiful."

That surprised me because I had often hiked past similar trees that were stunted and twisted into grotesque shapes by the fierce, cold winds that frequently buffet the peaks of Mount Mitchell. But when he showed me a box he had carved from this type of wood, I understood that what was once ugly and battered could be made into something exquisite by a masterful hand. I asked him to show me a piece of the rough wood.

"I haven't any right now. You see, I won't cut such trees down. I wait until they fall, and then I retrieve them and turn the wood into something beautiful."

Like those trees along our windswept mountain ridges, we often find ourselves buffeted by storms—the storms of life. We need deep roots that will supply us with the spiritual nutrients to grow strong in our faith and to keep us anchored when we are tossed about by life's trials.

God's Resources for Spiritual Growth

How do we grow strong in our faith? What spiritual resources has God given to make this happen?

The Bible. God's Word is given by God to teach us His truth and guide us through life. He says, "I am the LORD your God, who teaches you what is best for you, who directs you in the way you should go" (Isaiah 48:17).

How does this help us develop spiritually? First, it points us to the

God's truths are the constant rain that waters our root system of faith and nourishes our growing roots with principles to live by.

truth—about God, about ourselves, about the world around us, about the future, and most of all, about Jesus Christ and His love for us. His truths are the constant rain that waters our root system of faith and nourishes our growing roots with principles to live by.

Every day, we face decisions. How can we be sure we make the right ones? By applying biblical principles. The Bible gives us practical wisdom for daily living. It is our instructor, showing us how to live, and it's our authority in everything.

From one end to the other, God's Word is filled with promises—promises concerning His unchanging love, His presence, His help, His peace—in times of turmoil. Most of all, the Bible promises that someday we will go to be with God in heaven forever because of what Jesus Christ has done for us.

The Holy Spirit. He is the Source of power. When we come to Jesus Christ and put our faith and trust in Him, God Himself comes to live within us through His Holy Spirit. He isn't an impersonal force (like gravity). He is a person, just as God the Father and Christ the Son are persons—personal in their natures—so is the Holy Spirit, working and active in the lives of believers.

Why does God the Holy Spirit come to live within us when we give our lives to Christ? One reason is to assure us of our salvation. How do we know Christ has forgiven all our sins and given us the gift of eternal life? We know it because the Bible says so—and the Holy Spirit confirms in our hearts that this is true (Romans 8:16).

The Holy Spirit will help us discover God's will in our walk with Him. Certainly the Bible gives us principles to live by, helping us to avoid wrong and to do what is right. But often we face choices that seem equally good, and we need to know which is right. God wants to guide us as we make those choices because He loves us and wants us to have what is best.

The Holy Spirit encourages and strengthens us in times of trouble. "The Spirit helps us in our weakness" (Romans 8:26), and this includes more than just helping us as we pray. When hard times come, He may bring to mind passages of Scripture that assure us of God's love and protection. When temptations assail us, the Spirit strengthens us and gives us courage to fight our adversary, the devil.

Finally, the Holy Spirit has come to change us from within. God wants to change our lives, to make us more like Christ.

Prayer. Prayer is another resource for spiritual growth. Some people look on prayer as a burden or obligation, but in reality, it is one of our greatest privileges as God's children. Think of it—the God of the universe wants us to bring every concern to Him in prayer!

Does God always answer our prayers the way we wish He would? No, not necessarily—nor has He promised to do so. He knows what is best for us, even when we don't. That's why sometimes He says no or not now. But God has promised to hear us when we pray and to answer our prayers in His time

Think of it—the God of the universe wants us
to bring every concern to Him in prayer!

GOD'S STRENGTH FOR HARD TIMES

and in His way. Remember, however, that prayer isn't just asking for things we want.

Speaking to the Lord is important for every moment of our lives, not just for times of suffering or joy. True prayer includes thanking and praising Him for who He is and all He does. According to 1 Thessalonians 5:17, our minds and hearts should constantly be in an attitude of prayer as we "pray continually." Really, prayer is a place, a place where we meet God in genuine conversation.

Other Believers. We are not meant to be isolated from and independent of each other, either as human beings or as Christians. We need other people in our lives, and they need us. This is especially true as we seek to grow in faith. A solitary Christian is inevitably a weak Christian because he or she is failing to draw strength from what God is doing in the lives of fellow brothers and sisters in Christ.

If you aren't currently part of an active group of believers, ask God to guide you to a church where you can grow in your faith through biblical preaching and teaching and worship. The church is a storehouse of spiritual food. This is where our souls are fed, nourished, and developed into maturity. It is there we can "encourage one another and build each other up" (1 Thessalonians 5:11).

God wants to use you right where you are. Every day you probably come into contact with people who will never enter a church or talk with a pastor or open a Bible. You may be the bridge God uses to bring them to His Son, the

Lord Jesus Christ. Anyone can be a servant, no matter how inadequate he or she may feel.

Planted in Fertile Soil

I recall a neighbor in my community wanted a tree to shade the hot eastern corner of her home. A young purple-leaf plum tree seemed the perfect choice, but it was not. Five years after planting, the tree was stunted—frequently attacked by insects and struck with blights—and worse, any strong wind would make it lean until its branches touched the ground. No matter how she staked it, it would not stand tall against the elements. She complained about this to a friend, so he examined the tree and identified the problem—it had never taken root. Planted close to a downspout, the tree never needed to stretch its roots beyond its infant root ball to find water. It eventually would die.

Contrast this tree with the maple sapling planted on the edge of her property the same spring. A bare-root plant, the sapling was forced to reach up for sun and out for water. Five years later, it was taller and healthier than the stunted plum tree.

The Christian life should look like the life cycle of that maple sapling. After our roots of faith are planted in the fertile soil of truth, we should grow strong as we understand God's Word, draw close to the Holy Spirit, talk to God daily in prayer, and fellowship with others in Christ. As we drink from the springs of life, our roots will grow deeper when we are obedient to Christ. Only with a deep root system can we endure the storms of life.

As we drink from the springs of life, our roots will grow deeper when we are obedient to Christ.

Two

GOD STRENGTHENS THE
YOUNG AND THE AGED

He gives strength to the weary and increases the power of the weak.

Isaiah 40:29

―――――――

People have told me over the years that they believe God speaks through His Word, but they don't believe He actually hears their pleas. Scripture dispels this. For those who fear and honor the Lord, He hears the voice of weeping (Psalm 6:8) and says, "Refrain your voice from weeping, and your eyes from tears; for your work shall be rewarded. . . . There is hope in your future" (Jeremiah 31:16–17 NKJV).

If you feel weak, listen for God's words of comfort: "Hear my voice" (Isaiah 28:23), and "Lift up your voice with strength" (Isaiah 40:9 NKJV). He hears the voice of your words (Deuteronomy 5:28) and attends to your voice in prayer (Psalm 66:19). I hope these reminders from Scripture boost your spirit.

One of my great surprises in the aging process has been the loss of strength to do the simplest things, and to lose hearing, vision, and strength of voice. These senses weaken as the years pass. But old age has its compensations. One is reflecting on God's goodness over the years and giving us opportunities to assure others that God truly is faithful to His promises, demonstrated through our own experiences. We shouldn't think about ourselves and how weak we are. Instead, we should think about God and how strong He is. We can ask God to strengthen us and help us reflect Christ as we grow older. Life is hard—but God is good, and life can grow sweeter and more rewarding as we age if we possess the presence of Christ. The psalmist wrote of this: "My flesh and my heart may fail, but God is the strength of my heart" (Psalm 73:26). Are we depending on Him?

Our dependence on God delights Him. Paul reminds us in Colossians 1:29 that he depended on Christ's mighty power that works within, and we can claim this as well. Remember, God didn't create our bodies to live forever, and He knows exactly how we feel. He also created the glorious sunset and adds colors, glory, and beauty to the sunset of life. We must learn to listen to His voice and follow Him. Are we recognizing His voice?

I long to hear His voice and see Christ face-to-face. In the day I go to be with Him, there will be no unfulfilled longings or disappointments. He will welcome me into His heavenly home and teach me the wisdom of the ages. But we don't have to wait to hear His voice in heaven—we can hear His voice today. The Bible says that He sends out His mighty voice and we can hear it (Psalm 68:33; 95:7).

We shouldn't think about ourselves and how weak we are.
Instead, we should think about God and how strong He is.

Recognizing the Voice of God

I have never heard the voice of the Lord audibly, but the Lord has spoken to me many times throughout my life. You might ask, "How can someone recognize His voice?" The Bible says, "Everyone on the side of truth listens to me" (John 18:37). To recognize the voice of the Lord, we must belong to Him.

My wife, Ruth, never had to identify herself when she called me on my many trips around the world. When I picked up the phone and heard her speak, I knew her voice. I never had to ask my children to identify themselves by name when they phoned. My sisters and my brother were unmistakable voices to me. We recognize the voices of those who are dear to us and those with whom we commune.

Likewise, if we are communicating with the Lord Jesus through prayer and meditating on His Word, our spirits will identify with His voice. Jesus said, "My sheep listen to my voice; I know them, and they follow me" (John 10:27). The Bible says, "I will give them hearts that recognize me as the LORD" (Jeremiah 24:7 NLT), and "Obey My voice, and I will be your God" (Jeremiah 7:23 NKJV).

The voice of the Lord comes in various ways: a voice in the midst of the fire (Deuteronomy 5:24), a voice upon the waters (Psalm 29:3), a voice from heaven (Matthew 3:17), a voice out of the cloud (Matthew 17:5), the voice of His mouth (Acts 22:14), a voice from the excellent glory (2 Peter 1:17 KJV), and a voice out of the throne (Revelation 19:5).

God's voice is not bound by man's inventions.

God speaks to the human heart.

Do we listen for His voice in our everyday activities? Sometimes He speaks, but we don't hear. God's voice is not bound by man's inventions. God speaks to the human heart. His voice is described as full of majesty (Psalm 29:4), a still small voice (1 Kings 19:12 NKJV), and a glorious voice (Isaiah 30:30). The Lord's voice is identified as the voice of the living God (Deuteronomy 5:26), the voice of the bridegroom (Jeremiah 7:34), and the voice of the Almighty (Ezekiel 1:24).

His is a powerful voice (Psalm 29:4). It shakes the wilderness (Psalm 29:8 NKJV), divides the flames of fire (Psalm 29:7 NKJV), thunders (Job 37:5), and rushes like many waters (Revelation 1:15 NKJV). His voice cries to the city (Micah 6:9 NKJV). We are to obey His voice (Deuteronomy 13:4) and His Word (Psalm 103:20). If we will stop and listen with our ears and our hearts, we will hear God's voice.

It used to be that when I would get on an airplane, my wife would be assured she wouldn't hear from me for hours. Telecommunications have changed our world. Now there are few instances when anyone is disconnected. We can call from the sky while in flight. It is no longer necessary to pull off the highway to make a call from a pay phone. But sometimes reception is difficult. It is not unusual for a cellular phone to drop a call midsentence or for the transmission to be interrupted momentarily because of interference.

If God did not want to commune with us, then He would not question man;

but not only does He want to communicate with us, He wants us to speak His name in prayer.

The first question God asked man was, "Where are you?" Adam answered, "I heard Your voice in the garden" (Genesis 3:9–10 NKJV). Sometimes we don't want to hear what He has to say because we already know what the Word of God has told us. The Bible is full of accounts of men and women hearing the voice of the Lord but not recognizing it at first. This happened to the prophet Samuel. God called him by name, over and over. Samuel thought it was someone else. But the Lord persisted until Samuel recognized His voice (1 Samuel 3:10).

He also wants to hear from us. He expects a response. Isaiah "heard the voice of the Lord saying, 'Whom shall I send?'" Isaiah responded, "Here am I! Send me" (Isaiah 6:8 NKJV). The persecutor of Christians heard the voice of the Lord saying, "Saul, Saul, why are you persecuting Me?" In this remarkable exchange, Saul responded, "Who are You, Lord? . . . What do You want me to do?" (Acts 9:4–6 NKJV). This dialogue was the beginning of the apostle Paul's great ministry.

God is a loving God who cares about our needs. His voice gives comfort and guidance. Gideon heard the Lord speak peace (Judges 6:23), and Habakkuk heard God's voice say, "The righteous person will live by his faithfulness" (Habakkuk 2:4).

God is a loving God who cares about our needs.
His voice gives comfort and guidance.

The Fountain of Life versus the Fountain of Youth

It took me a while to grasp this great and wonderful truth. As a young man, my head resisted what my soul longed for. My hardened soul was redeemed, and I exchanged my will for God's way. I heard the Gospel with my heart and answered His call.

While I choose not to dwell on the past or relive my youth, there are times I long to stand in the pulpit to deliver a Gospel message. But the walker, wheelchair, and cane near my bed remind me that chapter in life is past. So I thank God for the memories that have enriched my life and want to look forward to new experiences that can add some dimension to the present.

Young people live for today and search for new experiences; the "aged" yearn for the past and relive it in their minds. Oh, just to be young again! Juan Ponce de León, the Spanish explorer who traveled at one time with Christopher Columbus, went in search of a magic water source that people called the fountain of youth. Rumor had it that drinking its waters would keep one young. Ponce de León was determined to find this legendary fountain; instead he found Florida—what became America's retirement haven. How many couples have packed their belongings, pulled up roots, and left home and family to set up housekeeping in a condo on a Florida golf course—with a nursing home across the fairway?

The world's idea of a fountain of youth is a mirage. Only the Bible provides an oasis for the soul: "The fear of the LORD is a fountain of life" (Proverbs 14:27). To grasp the meaning of this verse, we must first understand what "fear of the Lord" means. It is contrary to being afraid of Him. God would not have sent His Son to earth to communicate with us if He wanted humanity to be fearful of approaching Him. This wonderful phrase throughout Scripture is a reminder to be in reverential awe of God, to love Him with our whole being and commit ourselves joyfully to Him in all things: "Love the LORD your God with all your heart and with all your soul and with all your strength" (Deuteronomy 6:5). The apostle John said it this way: "Keep away from anything that might take God's place in your hearts" (1 John 5:21 NLT).

God's Word gives us many wonderful pictures of fountains that flow with life-giving blessings: "For you [God] are the fountain of life, the light by which we see" (Psalm 36:9 NLT); "The words of the godly are a life-giving fountain" (Proverbs 10:11 NLT); "The instruction of the wise is like a life-giving fountain" (13:14 NLT); and "Discretion is a life-giving fountain" (16:22 NLT). Then the Lord Jesus sums it all up in the closing book of the Bible: "I am the Alpha and the Omega, the Beginning and the End. I will give of the fountain of the water of life freely to him who thirsts. He who overcomes shall inherit all things" (Revelation 21:6–7 NKJV).

The fountain of youth is only a dream, but the fountain of life is real, friends. We can draw strength from its resources and stand strong in our resolve to be

The world's idea of a fountain of youth is a mirage.
Only the Bible provides an oasis for the soul.

overcomers, looking forward to the inheritance and being in the presence of the Savior of our souls. Though the eyes of the tired, overworked, and aged may dim, God's light will pour into our hearts.

God's Strength in Our Weakness

Let the promises of God's Word, the Bible, uphold you every day. Turn constantly to Him in prayer, confident that not only does He hear you, but even now, Jesus is interceding for you. Focus your thoughts on Christ and maintain your connection with other believers who can encourage and help you. The Bible's words are true: "Neither death nor life, neither angels nor demons, neither the present nor the future . . . nor anything else in all creation, will be able to separate us from the love of God that is in Christ Jesus our Lord" (Romans 8:38–39).

In the weeks before her death, my wife repeated these verses over and over to us. Ruth was always thinking of others. This was her secret for getting through so much of life with joy. She never focused on her problems; she turned her attention to Christ, and He always led her to someone who needed a word of encouragement or a listening ear. The Lord blesses people who bless others, and He gives grace to those who focus on the things that please Him.

True joy is derived from depending on the Lord Jesus. He is the One who supplies our strength in weakness, for when we are weak, He is strong (2 Corinthians 12:10). We must not forget to make the things of God the center of our thinking and doing.

Are you concerned only about taking care of business in a world that holds you captive? Or are you setting Christ at the center of your life with the assurance that you will abide with Him for eternity—the place where hope becomes reality? Your strength may fade, but He is the One who will lift you up and help you stand strong in your weakness. When your faith begins to fade, ask the Lord to stir it up by considering all He has done for you and be strong, for "my Spirit remains among you" (Haggai 2:5).

Three

THE PRESENCE OF GOD'S
STRENGTH TO THE LONELY

Turn to me and be gracious to me, for I am lonely and afflicted.

PSALM 25:16

———

Loneliness has never been a respecter of persons; it intrudes into the lives of those who live in palaces, skyscrapers, the suburbs, and village huts. The world's greatest artists, writers, composers, kings and queens, and carpenters and plumbers experience loneliness. Movies depict the lives of so many lonely people. Some of the loneliest people are famous; they are in a world to themselves.

Are you lonely?

A professor of psychology says there are two basic causes of loneliness: the feeling that we don't belong and the feeling that no one understands us. If I could ask, "Are you lonely?" the answer from many would be yes. Even in a large crowd, we can feel alone. When we go home, even if our family is there, sometimes loneliness remains. Why? Because we're lonely for God. We were made in the image of God, for fellowship with Him.

God didn't create Adam and Eve because He was lonely, as some say. God is complete in Himself; He lacks nothing. But He makes it possible for us to have an abundant life in Him. So what makes us lonely?

Mobility and constant change tend to make some individuals feel rootless and disconnected. Loneliness is also a principal cause of both alcoholism and drug abuse as an effort to escape it. But it doesn't work. Loneliness creeps in because something is missing from our lives. Too often, we've neglected our spirit, leaving us lonely and searching to fill a void.

What we need is reconciliation to God. Before we accept Christ, we're separated from God. Scripture teaches that we were sinners even in our mother's womb (Psalm 51:5). We're all sinners; we've broken the laws of God, and we're born with that tendency. How do we bridge the gap?

We need to come to the cross and bring our sins to Jesus for forgiveness and redemption—and leave them there. It was on the cross that Christ died for our sins and shed His blood. He takes the two arms of the cross, wraps them around us, and says, "I love you."

All Kinds of Lonely

There are several kinds of loneliness. There's the *loneliness of society*. Homeless people are everywhere. I once gave a man on Fifth Avenue some money at

Christ takes the two arms of the cross, wraps them around us, and says, "I love you."

Christmastime, and I asked him what his main problem was. He said, "I'm so alone."

Jesus once looked at a paralyzed man who said, "Sir . . . I have no one to help me" (John 5:7). Thirty-eight years he was alone, until Jesus singled him out. He became that man's friend that day, and He healed him. He can become your friend.

After Dwight Eisenhower became president of the United States, he was asked what his favorite hymn was, and he responded, "What a Friend We Have in Jesus." He knew he needed a friend.

I remember when he invaded Normandy. He stood on the coast of England up on a bluff, and his head was bowed. He sent me a picture of that years later, and he wrote, "I found a friend, and that friend is Jesus."

Loneliness is found even in the intimacy of marriage. But even in the midst of that love, some feel so alone. A marriage based only on physical attraction or romantic emotions may be doomed to failure right from the start.

Loneliness is an inner dimension. It's a thirst for the Spirit for God. You may not recognize it as a thirst for God, but that's what it is. The Bible says your mind, your body, your soul, and your spirit—made in the image of God—are thirsty for Him. The roots of loneliness are in each of us.

There is also the *loneliness of suffering*. Christ gives us hope that suffering is going to come to an end and we'll exchange the suffering on earth for the glory of heaven! The apostle Paul said, "I consider that our present sufferings are not worth comparing with the glory that will be revealed in us" (Romans 8:18).

Revelation 21:4 says, "He will wipe every tear from their eyes. There will be no more death or mourning or crying or pain, for the old order of things has passed away."

Then there's the *loneliness of sorrow*. Jesus wept at the funeral of a friend. He said, "I am the resurrection and the life. The one who believes in me will live, even though they die; and whoever lives by believing in me will never die" (John 11:25–26). That's the hope He gives to those who are suffering in sorrow.

I wasn't with either of my parents when they died, but I arrived shortly after, and there was the loneliness of sorrow. No matter where I had been in the world, it was a comfort to know they had been praying for me.

If a friend of yours or a loved one has died, Jesus is the resurrection and the life. If they knew Christ, He will raise that person up. That is our hope and certainty.

The deeper and more basic root of loneliness is a sense of isolation from God. Do you know when loneliness began? In the garden of Eden when man cut himself off from fellowship with God. Adam rebelled against God, and from that moment on, he became a sinner, and sin has been passed down from generation to generation—to you and me.

In the garden of Eden, man and woman lived together in perfect harmony

If a friend of yours or a loved one has died, Jesus is the resurrection and the life. If they knew Christ, He will raise that person up. That is our hope and certainty.

with each other and with God. Then something devastating happened. There was a declaration of independence. They said, "Lord, we don't need You any longer. We can build our world without You." So they declared their independence of Him. God came to the garden, calling, "Adam, where are you?" They tried to hide from God, like you and I try to hide from God, but there's no hiding place. The roots of loneliness were planted in the human soul and have been inherited by everyone since.

We are born in sin. We sin by choice, and we're sinners by nature. Sin separates us from God, and only Christ's death on the cross can reconcile us to Him. We have to come to the cross and acknowledge that we're sinners, and that we are ready to change our way of living. That's called repentance.

Perhaps there was a time when you knew the fellowship of God. You walked with Him. You went to church. You read the Bible. You were faithful in the way you lived. But now gradually you've been weaned away, and you don't walk as close to the Lord as you once did. You went out from the presence of the Lord, and you found that it was night. In John 13, we read the story of the Last Supper and the portrayal of Judas. He went out, the Scripture says, and "it was night." He betrayed the Lord, and he was lonely, having no fellowship with Christ from that point forward.

But you can come back. Jesus stands with open arms. He says, "Come back. I love you. I receive you. I will forgive you." He waits for you to make that decision. You cannot depend upon others to make a decision for Christ. You have to make it yourself.

Jesus Knows the Pain of Loneliness

Jesus spent much time in the company of the lonely and the outcast. Even though great crowds surrounded Him at times, He was alone. Scripture says that, at the end, everyone, even the disciples, "deserted him and fled" (Mark 14:50). The crowds who had shouted "Hosanna" earlier that very week began to shout, "Crucify Him. Crucify Him." He was alone.

At the last, we hear Him crying from the cross, "My God, my God, why have you forsaken me?" (Mark 15:34). Christ, hanging on the cross, was lonely. Why? Because as He shed His blood and bore your sins and mine on the cross, the Bible tells us that God, who cannot look upon sin, turned His face from His Son. It seemed at that moment that even the Father had forsaken Him. He was enduring the penalty of death for you and me. He took our judgment. That's how much He loves us. He doesn't want us to be lonely and separated from Him. He wants us to come back to Him.

Jesus Christ experienced ultimate loneliness when He died, but through His death, He dealt with the primary cause of human loneliness: separation from

Jesus stands with open arms. He says, "Come back.
I love you. I receive you. I will forgive you."

God. With one arm from the cross, He held on to the hand of the Father. With the other, He reaches out to you.

Jesus Is the Remedy for Loneliness

There are multitudes of lonely people who carry heavy and difficult burdens, but the loneliest of all is one whose life is steeped in sin. Our reaction to loneliness is often to deal with the symptoms rather than the cause. We get involved in our work, consumed in our pleasures. We throw ourselves into a social whirl to escape the loneliness that's there, but somehow it doesn't work. If we search for an antidote to loneliness, we often end up deeper in the quicksand and worse off than we were before. We spin out of control.

But any attempt to deal with sin without the new birth is like struggling in quicksand. There's no remedy in this life except Christ. Through Him, we can have the most important relationship in life restored. The things that are broken in our hearts and lives can be restored when we put our faith and confidence in Christ.

"Here I am! I stand at the door and knock," Jesus says. "If anyone hears my voice and opens the door, I will come in and eat with that person, and they with me" (Revelation 3:20). The psalmist, who was also lonely, wrote in Psalm 43:5,

"Why, my soul, are you downcast? Why so disturbed within me? Put your hope in God, for I will yet praise him, my Savior and my God." Yes, you can smile again. You can have the joy of the Lord in your heart.

Loneliness is often God's way of letting us know that it's time to come back to Him. Christ experienced the greatest loneliness the world has ever known so that we would never have to be lonely again. With Christ as your Savior and constant Companion, you need never be lonely.

Four

GOD'S STRENGTH BRINGS
CONTENTMENT

Godliness with contentment is great gain. For we brought nothing into the world, and we can take nothing out of it.

1 TIMOTHY 6:6–7

Becoming a Christian takes only a single step; being a Christian means walking with Christ the rest of your life. True faith and suffering frequently go hand in hand. Living for Christ, walking in His way, will not be an easy path.

We have at our fingertips every pleasure that man is capable of enjoying, and we have abused every gift God ever gave us. We have allowed worldly desires and pleasures to fill the heart and mind. The world is mad in its obsession with pleasure, sex, and money. Its ear is too dull to hear the truth. Eyes are blind; they do not want to see. They hurry to their doom.

Many people have no appetite for spiritual things because they are absorbed in the sinful pleasures of this world. Our lust for immediate pleasure prompts us to think of evil as good. The more worldly pleasure we enjoy, the less satisfied and contented we are with life. As for the world system of evil, we are to be separated from it.

This then is our problem: How can we associate with and love those who

The greatest roadblock to Satan's work is the Christian who lives for God, walks with integrity, is filled with the Spirit, and finds contentment in obeying Him in all things.

are involved in the world without being contaminated, influenced, or swayed by them? There are so many professing Christians who are walking hand in hand with the world that it's impossible to tell the difference between the Christian and the unbeliever. This should never be!

The Christian way of daily living must be distinct from the world. This can only be achieved by a close walk with Christ, by constant prayer, and by seeking the Holy Spirit's leadership every hour of the day. We are in the world, but the world is not to be in us. The greatest roadblock to Satan's work is the Christian who, above all else, lives for God, walks with integrity, is filled with the Spirit, and finds contentment in obeying Him in all things.

Can we be content in walking with Christ, and if so, how? "Delight yourself also in the LORD, and He shall give you the desires of your heart" (Psalm 37:4 NKJV). Christ takes away all the stuff that weighs us down and implants a longing for us to do His will.

We must also learn to shut out the distractions that keep us from truly worshiping God. This is not about standing in church one hour a week and singing. Worship in the truest sense takes place only when our full attention is on God—on giving Him glory in all things, in praying for His power to strengthen us, and by our obedience to walk in His way.

To be a disciple of Christ is to be committed to Him as Savior and Lord and to be disciplined in our bodies, minds, and souls. The true child of God will have a hunger for worship and God's Word: "He who heeds the word wisely will find good . . . happy is he" (Proverbs 16:20 NKJV).

When I was busy traveling from city to city, country to country, for weeks and months at a time, I remember how wonderful it was to have a few days of relaxation at my home in North Carolina. I would walk the mountain trails, ride horseback, and do some of the things I hadn't done perhaps in a year or more. This gave me an opportunity to spend time with the Lord in the solitude of the mountains. It gave me a chance to be with my wife and hike with my children. It allowed me time to dwell on the values of life, and to study the Scriptures without distraction. How good it would be for everyone to go out to the country from time to time, to stand beside a fast-moving stream or sit in a quiet little glen and think. So few of us take the time to do this.

A study once surveyed a cross-section of people asking to identify the real values of life. More than half said the most important value is economic security, followed by liberty, freedom, and then world peace. Less than 10 percent named education, religion, decency, morality, and being a good citizen.

Now, all of those things are excellent, but I was shocked that religion was such a small priority. Most people, it seemed, were more interested in where they were headed, the clothes they were going to wear, and their financial securities. Students want to be independent and on their own, but you'll find them

How good it would be for everyone to
go out to the country from time to time,
to stand beside a fast-moving stream or
sit in a quiet little glen and think.

conforming to their environment and their peers. Then there are those who strive for a good job with a big firm and a home in the suburbs. But still they don't find security. Their values are misplaced.

True Wealth

Contrary to public opinion, Jesus says there are certain things in life more important than economic security. Spiritual values should come first:

Therefore I tell you, do not worry about your life, what you will eat or drink; or about your body, what you will wear. Is not life more than food, and the body more than clothes? Look at the birds of the air; they do not sow or reap or store away in barns, and yet your heavenly Father feeds them. Are you not much more valuable than they? Can any one of you by worrying add a single hour to your life? And why do you worry about clothes? See how the flowers of the field grow. They do not labor or spin. Yet I tell you that not even Solomon in all his splendor was dressed like one of these. If that is how God clothes the grass of the field, which is here today and tomorrow is thrown into the fire, will he not much more clothe you—you of little faith? So do not worry, saying, "What shall we eat?" or

"What shall we drink?" or "What shall we wear?" For the pagans run after all these things, and your heavenly Father knows that you need them. But seek first his kingdom and his righteousness, and all these things will be given to you as well. (Matthew 6:25–33)

If the average person were asked, "What is the most important thing in life?" many would answer "wealth." Some strive to pile up money for old age. In time they find that the strain of getting the money has caused ulcers or some other disease, and they're not able to enjoy their fortunes, big or small. They're breaking their health to meet their goals while neglecting their families and forgetting to live.

Jesus warned us to "guard against all kinds of greed; life does not consist in an abundance of possessions" (Luke 12:15). A person can be a millionaire and be poor toward God; God counts them as poverty stricken. The only rich people in the world are those who know God, who know Christ, because Jesus Christ said that these material things do not bring permanent happiness or contentment. The Bible warns that money cannot buy happiness: "Don't love money; be satisfied with what you have" (Hebrews 13:5 NLT). When we are consumed with attaining the pot of gold and every kind of pleasure, our minds are not on Christ.

The only rich people in the world
are those who know God.

True Provision

Scripture mentions gold more than any other metal, first in its description of the lands surrounding Eden (Genesis 2:11–12). In Haggai 2:8, God says "the gold is mine." Though it was highly valued, it was used abundantly in making things from cups to crowns, shields to bells, vessels to scepters, altars to thrones, and door hinges to streets. The Bible speaks of choice gold, precious gold, fine gold, perfect gold, threads of gold, weights of gold, talents of gold, pure gold, dust of gold, and cherubim of gold.

But gold wasn't used just for divine purposes. Men also melted the precious metal to form idols. They unwisely valued gold more than they valued God. Scripture teaches that virtues such as wisdom, knowledge, reputation, and faith are valued more than gold: "I, wisdom, dwell with prudence, and find out knowledge and discretion. . . . Counsel is mine, and sound wisdom; I am understanding, I have strength. . . . And those who seek me diligently will find me. Riches and honor are with me, enduring riches and righteousness. My fruit is better than gold, yes, than fine gold" (Proverbs 8:12, 14, 17–19 NKJV).

Jesus didn't leave a material inheritance to His disciples. He willed His followers something more valuable than gold. He willed us His peace. He said, "My peace I give to you; not as the world gives" (John 14:27 NKJV).

The Lord places a high value on the virtues of wisdom, knowledge, a good name, and faith. These are just a few of the many attributes of God, and He offers them to those who live for Him. "All the things one may desire cannot be compared with [wisdom]" (Proverbs 8:11 NKJV). In Proverbs 16:16 we are told that it is "much better to get wisdom than gold!" (NKJV). "There is gold and a multitude of rubies, but the lips of knowledge are a precious jewel" (Proverbs 20:15 NKJV). "A good name is to be chosen rather than great riches, loving favor rather than silver and gold. The rich and the poor have this in common, the LORD is the maker of them all" (Proverbs 22:1–2 NKJV). "Faith [is] much more precious than gold" (1 Peter 1:7 NKJV).

True Happiness

If you ask the average person what else is basic in life, he or she may answer happiness. So we spend billions of dollars to amuse ourselves. America has the greatest variety and number of artificial amusements of any country. People have become so empty that they can't even entertain themselves. With every source of amusement pouring poison into daily life, it's no wonder that the minds of people are ready to receive anything but the truth and ready to believe lies in order to attain happiness.

Certainly we may have times of leisure and relaxation, yet Jesus taught that neither were the first thing nor the basic thing in life. We'll never find happiness by looking for it. We can try every amusement available. We can run after every type of entertainment that has been invented and still not find what we're looking for. Why? Because basic happiness is not found in these things—they only give momentary pleasure.

Some men, women, and young people have become enslaved to the god of pleasure. We must have our pleasures. We must be entertained constantly. Others have become slaves to ambition—get ahead, be somebody important, have power. Still others have become slaves to every social ill of the day.

I once asked a man, "You have enough money at sixty-five years of age; why don't you retire and give up this obsession with money?" He said, "I can't. I've been making money all my life. It's become a habit with me. I'm a slave to it."

We're busy chasing after other gods instead of serving the true and living God by personal faith in Christ. How can we do this? Scripture tells us, "Christ also suffered for us, leaving us an example, that you should follow His steps" (1 Peter 2:21 NKJV).

These various sins bind us in ropes and chains because they've become our gods. They take the place of God in our life and, as a result, we find ourselves refusing to give up our other gods and put Christ at the center of life. But I want to tell you that Jesus Christ can cut the ropes and chains that bind us.

I have met a lot of people in Hollywood and on Broadway. I've met congressmen, senators, and members of Parliament who have risen to the very top. They've had all the amusement, glamour, and prestige that money, fame, and power can buy. They've seen their names in bright lights. But many of them are miserable. A young Hollywood star once bowed his head in my presence and started crying. He said, "Billy, I made a fortune, my name is known around the world, but I'm a most unhappy man in the world because all of these things have not satisfied the longing of my heart."

True Health

Something else important to most everyone is health. We say, "If I can just keep a good strong body; if I can keep young and vigorous . . ." I know a lady who is fifty years old who goes to a plastic surgeon twice a year. She's trying to hold on to her youth. But the wrinkles will come, and she will grow old. Our health is always in jeopardy—even for the young person who is in perfect health, it can change in a moment. Someday life will be over for everyone, no matter how much attention you give to your health. Will you look back with regret because you nourished your body but starved your soul?

There's something more important than physical health, and that is spiritual health. Don't allow yourself to be deceived!

When you let Jesus Christ into your heart and give
Him control, you've found your search is over.

We are like a restless sea, finding a little peace here and a little pleasure there, but nothing satisfies. Sin is the cause; sins are the effect. Sin is the tree; sins are the fruit. Sin is the disease; sins are the symptoms. The sin of self-pleasure is a deadly sin. How do we get our values so mixed up?

We humans have a longing in our hearts way down deep. There is an aching void in the soul. We think that something else is the answer so we are going in for a thrill, sowing our wild oats and kicking up our heels. We're searching for permanent happiness. I want to tell you, it can't be found that way.

No one has ever found it that way. The only truly happy people in the world are those who know Christ as personal Savior. When you let Jesus Christ into your heart and give Him control, you've found your search is over. The Bible says, "Humbly accept the word God has planted in your hearts, for it has the power to save your souls" (James 1:21 NLT).

Jesus said, "Consider how the wild flowers grow. They do not labor or spin. Yet I tell you, not even Solomon in all his splendor was dressed like one of these" (Luke 12:27). Do we really believe this? Jesus taught that utter dependence on God, utter dependence upon Christ, is the main thing, the real thing in life. The important thing is to know that you have peace with God, to know that your soul is right with Him.

All fear, frustration, conflict, difficulty, and problems can be solved when we call on the name of the Lord Jesus. He strengthens us and instructs us to turn our backs on sin, to no longer practice the ungodly patterns of living. Whoever you are, whatever your circumstances, your life can be changed by Christ, and you can experience the contentment and joy that He has for you.

Five

GOD STRENGTHENS THROUGH PRAYER AND PRAISE

Do not be anxious about anything, but in every situation, by prayer and petition, with thanksgiving, present your requests to God.

PHILIPPIANS 4:6

———

There is one thing that all of us can do in hard times: we can pray. Prayer to our Father in heaven should be the very first thing we do—not the last resort. What a tremendous privilege we have to approach the throne of God in prayer. If you feel intimidated by prayer, you are not alone, but don't let it silence you. Kneel in humbleness, look up in awe, fold your hands in thanksgiving, raise your hearts in praise, but pray. This is a gift from God to His children; this is how we commune with God, our Father in heaven.

Jesus' disciples—the men upon whose shoulders rested the responsibility of evangelizing the world—came to Jesus with one supreme request. They did not say, "Lord, teach us to preach" or "Lord, teach us to do miracles" or "Lord, teach us to be wise."

What did they say? "Lord, teach us to pray" (Luke 11:1). Where do you suppose they learned the supreme importance of prayer? From Jesus.

He considered prayer more important than food, for the Bible says, "Very

Prayer is a gift from God to His children; this is how
we commune with God, our Father in heaven.

early in the morning, while it was still dark, Jesus got up, left the house and went off to a solitary place, where he prayed" (Mark 1:35).

Prayer was more important to the Son of God than the assembling of great throngs. The Bible says, "Yet the news about him spread all the more, so that crowds of people came to hear him and to be healed of their sicknesses. But Jesus often withdrew to lonely places and prayed" (Luke 5:15–16).

The precious hours of fellowship with His heavenly Father meant much more to our Savior than sleep. The Bible says, "Jesus went out to a mountainside to pray, and spent the night praying to God" (Luke 6:12). We can do the same, but do we?

Heaven is full of answers to prayer for which no one ever bothered to ask. If there were any tears shed in heaven, they would be over the fact that we prayed so little. Prayer is for every moment of our lives, not just for times of suffering. Prayer is also to rejoice and offer thanks to God for His blessings. It is our lifeline to God. True prayer is a way of life for the Christian. How sad when we only pray in cases of emergencies. Prayer should not be merely an act but an attitude of life, for this is how we meet with God in genuine conversation.

A friend of mine defines prayer as a "declaration of dependence." Many times I have been driven to prayer. When I was in Bible school, I didn't know what to do with my life. I used to walk the streets and pray, sometimes for hours at a time. In His timing, God answered those prayers, and since then it has been an essential part of my life. Prayer strengthens me in weakness. Prayer guides me when my steps are uncertain. Prayer lifts me up when I'm discouraged. I've never met anyone who was strong in faith and spent time in daily prayer and the study of God's Word who was discouraged for very long.

Where do we start? How do we start? The book of Psalms is the Bible's hymnbook. It shows what it means to walk with God in prayer and praise. In the morning, prayer is the key that opens to us the treasures of God's mercies and blessings. In the evening, it is the key that shuts us up under His protection and safeguard. No matter where we are, God is as close as a prayer. He is our support and our strength. We should pray that we will be emptied of self and be placed completely at His disposal.

Why Pray?

Pray because Christ died to give us access to the Father.

Pray because God is worthy of our praise.

Pray because we need His forgiveness, cleansing, guidance, and protection.

Pray because others need our prayers.

God urges us to bring our concerns to Him—not just petitions about our own needs but also intercessions for others. Many doctors today prescribe yoga

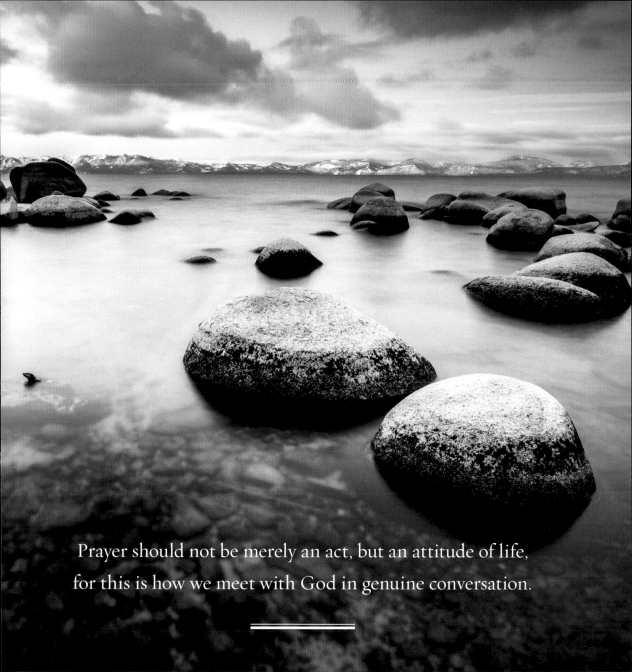

Prayer should not be merely an act, but an attitude of life,
for this is how we meet with God in genuine conversation.

Before prayer changes
others, it first changes us.

as a helpful stress reliever but would not consider prescribing prayer to the One who calms our fears and anxieties.

So why pray? Because the Christian life is a journey, and we need God's strength and guidance along the way. Before prayer changes others, it first changes us. When we are unsure whether or not something is wrong, we can ask ourselves: Does this glorify God? Can I offer a prayer of thanksgiving for it?

Prayer Moves Mountains

It has pleased God to relate His work in the world to the prayers of His people. Jesus Himself prayed at funerals, and the dead were raised (John 11:41–44). He prayed over the five loaves and two fishes, and a multitude was fed with a little boy's lunch (Matthew 14:19). He prayed, "Not as I will, but as you will" (26:39). And then in obedience, the Son of God went to the cross to make salvation possible for sinners.

We read of the patriarchs and the apostles who were empowered by God through prayer. Moses prayed, and God, amid thunder and lightning, etched His law on two tablets of stone. Gideon prayed, and the host of a formidable army fled in fear before his valiant, prayerful three hundred. David prayed, and he defeated the invincible Goliath on the Philistine battleground. Solomon prayed, and fire came down from heaven and consumed the burnt offerings and the sacrifices. Elijah prayed, and the fire of God consumed the sacrifice and licked up the water around the altar of the Baal prophets, to their consternation. Daniel prayed, and the mouths of lions closed. The disciples prayed, and they were filled with the Holy Spirit, and three thousand were added to the church in one day. Peter and John prayed, and a lame man was healed, and five thousand men and women believed.

"But effective prayer was for the ancients," people insist. "It has no relevance for this practical day." But nowhere in God's Word are we told that prayer was limited to a particular group or era. The Bible says, "Men always ought to pray and not lose heart" (Luke 18:1 NKJV).

Praying is more than an art or a skill—it is a consuming passion, the very life and breath of Christian living.

Many people have distorted ideas about what "praying in the Spirit" actually is, however. True prayer is not a muttering mumbo jumbo that makes God an errand runner, catering to our every selfish whim and desire. Real prayer is not a vain repetition of words uttered in public for religious display. Jesus said, "And when you pray, do not keep on babbling like pagans, for they think they will be heard because of their many words" (Matthew 6:7).

Prayer, in the true sense, is not a futile cry of desperation, born of fear. We know "there are no atheists in foxholes," but the kind of Christianity that fails

Praying is more than an art or a skill—
it is a consuming passion, the very life
and breath of Christian living.

to go beyond the foxhole into our everyday lives will never change the world. Prayer is not limited to conventional religious postures; it is not restricted to houses of worship or religious ceremony. The Bible says, "Therefore I want the men everywhere to pray, lifting up holy hands without anger or disputing" (1 Timothy 2:8).

Does Posture Matter?

Our physical posture is not so important as much as the attitude of the heart. Many people put a great deal of emphasis on the position that the body should be in while praying. Some insist that people kneel or fold the hands in a certain way. All of this is relatively unimportant, though kneeling is an act of humility when sincerely done.

Joshua "fell facedown to the ground in reverence" and prayed (Joshua 5:14). "Solomon stood before the altar of the LORD" (1 Kings 8:22). Three times a day, Daniel "got down on his knees and prayed" (Daniel 6:10). The disciples on the day of Pentecost "continued with one accord in prayer" when the Holy Spirit was outpoured on them (Acts 1:14 NKJV). Here we see four different positions that men of God used while praying.

Praying is simply a two-way conversation between you and God. The reason many people close their eyes while praying is in order to shut out the affairs of the world, enabling the mind to completely concentrate on conversation with God. However, nowhere in Scripture does it say that even the closing of the eyes is important, though it certainly lends itself to the attitude of prayer.

Who should pray and where should we pray? Scripture says that all are to pray (Luke 18:1) everywhere (1 Timothy 2:8 NKJV). While riding down the street in your car, you can pray. While walking down a boulevard, you can pray. While working at home, you can pray. Wherever you are, you can pray.

You may also ask, "When are we told to pray?" The Scripture says, "Continually" (1 Thessalonians 5:17). It is a command and a duty and a privilege to be always in the attitude of prayer.

Pray to the God Who Answers

First, *prayer is for God's children.* Jesus said, "When you pray, say, 'Our Father'" (Luke 11:2 NKJV).

Second, *prayer must be offered in faith.* The Bible says, "Therefore I tell you, whatever you ask for in prayer, believe that you have received it" (Mark 11:24). It goes without saying that if our prayers are aimless, meaningless, and mingled with doubt, they will go unanswered.

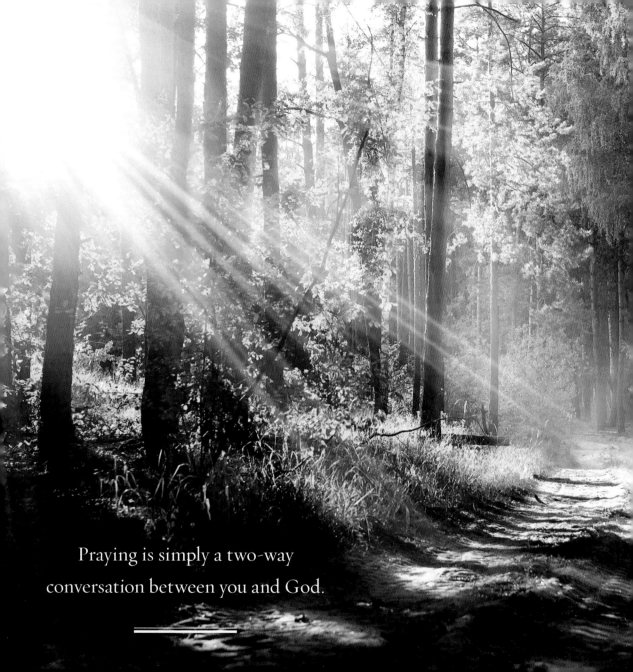

Praying is simply a two-way
conversation between you and God.

Third, *prayer must emanate from an obedient heart.* The Bible says, "Whatever we ask we receive from Him, because we keep His commandments and do those things that are pleasing in His sight" (1 John 3:22 NKJV).

Fourth, *we must pray in Christ's name.* Jesus said, "I will do whatever you ask in my name" (John 14:13). We are not worthy to approach the holy throne of God except through the Advocate, Jesus Christ.

Fifth, *we must pray in the will of God.* Even our Lord, contrary to His own disposition at the moment, said, "My Father, if it is not possible for this cup to be taken away unless I drink it, may your will be done" (Matthew 26:42).

And finally, *our prayers must be for God's glory.* The model prayer that Jesus has given us concludes with "Yours is the kingdom and the power and the glory" (Matthew 6:13 NKJV). If we have our prayers answered, we must give God the glory. Jesus said He answers our prayers "so that the Father may be glorified in the Son" (John 14:13).

What a privilege is ours—the privilege of prayer! Christian, examine your heart, consecrate your life, yield yourself to God unreservedly, for only those who pray through a clean heart will be heard by Him. The Bible says, "The prayer of a righteous person is powerful and effective" (James 5:16).

We must pray in times of adversity, lest we become faithless and unbelieving. Pray in times of prosperity, lest we become vaunted and proud. Pray in times of danger, lest we become fearful and doubting. Pray in times of security, lest we become self-sufficient.

Sinners, pray to a merciful God for forgiveness. Christians, pray for an outpouring of God's Spirit upon a willful, evil, unrepentant world. Parents, pray that God may crown your name with grace and mercy. Children, pray for the salvation of sin-chained parents. Christians, saints of God, pray that the dew of heaven may fall on earth's dry, thirsty ground and that righteousness may cover the earth as the waters cover the sea. Satan trembles when he sees the weakest saint upon his knees, so I beg of you, pray!

The way to God is through prayer. Ask God to forgive your sins in Christ's name, and if you are surrendering to Him as Lord and Savior, then for the first time in your life, you can have prayer answered.

You will never know peace of conscience, peace of mind, and peace of soul until you stand at the foot of the cross and, in prayer, submit your life to Christ and receive Him. This is peace with God, for God Himself is the power that makes prayer work.

What a privilege is ours—the privilege of prayer! ... The Bible says, "The prayer of a righteous person is powerful and effective" (James 5:16)

Six

—

GOD'S STRENGTH
OVERCOMES STORMS

These things I have spoken
to you, that in Me you may
have peace. In the world
you will have tribulation;
but be of good cheer, I have
overcome the world.

JOHN 16:33 NKJV

Believers must be prepared to face the storms of life on the stage of an unbelieving world because they will come. What are these storms? Temptation, confusion and despair, guilt, rejection, hopelessness, fear of death—to name just a few. These are the personal storms of life that we all face.

Then there are storms that jolt the world: famine, war, disease, tsunamis, and so on. None of these things takes God by surprise. He is in control no matter what comes. God has given us warning to prepare for storms, and certainly the storms that will come at the end of time, the Apocalypse. This scares even some believers, but Christians should take courage when they hear, "Trouble ahead, prepare to meet thy God." Are you prepared? Listen to what else the Lord declares. The voice of the gentle Shepherd says, "Come!" A new world is coming, and those in Christ will be there. The paradise that man lost will be regained. One day we will live in a brand-new world.

Are we prepared for the storms? Belonging to Jesus Christ is the first and

I've read the last page in the Bible, and it's all going to come out on God's side.

most crucial step. The next steps are a lifelong walk with God; getting to know Him and being able to call on Him are vital in storing up for life's storms that will surely come.

While in a restaurant some time ago, I overheard people at another table debating pessimism and optimism. One of the men recognized me and said, "Mr. Graham, are you an optimist or a pessimist?" I said, "I'm an optimist." He said, "Why?" I responded, "Because I've read the last page in the Bible, and it's all going to come out on God's side." God is going to win in the end, even though sometimes it doesn't seem like it.

Jesus said there would be a time upon the earth when there would be "distress of nations, with perplexity" (Luke 21:25 NKJV). Now, that word *distress* means pressure. Maybe you aren't pressured by world events, but you are pressured in your own life. You're pressured in your own family, in your work. Maybe you're pressured by the heavy load of guilt you carry.

I was riding in a taxi in New York City once when the cab driver turned to me and said, "Do you know anything that makes a fellow cheer a little, besides a glass of beer?" And I said, "Yes. I know something that can give you cheer. There was a Man who lived two thousand years ago, and four times He said, 'Be of good cheer.'" Jesus knew that He was to be executed. His country was overrun by a foreign power. And yet, four times He said, "Be of good cheer."

Your Sins Are Forgiven

The first time Jesus said that is found in Matthew 9:2: "Son, be of good cheer; your sins are forgiven you" (NKJV). A man who was sick with the palsy had been brought to Him. The man wanted to be healed, but Jesus looked down into his heart and saw a deeper need than physical healing. Jesus saw that he had a heart of sin, a heart of guilt.

Now, the sin and guilt had not caused the palsy. But the man had a deeper need, the need of every human being in the world. The Bible says, "All have sinned and fall short of the glory of God" (Romans 3:23).

Every one of us is infected with a fatal disease—a disease that will kill you three times because the Bible talks about three kinds of death. There's physical death as a result of sin: "People are destined to die once, and after that to face judgment" (Hebrews 9:27).

But there's another death, called spiritual death, and that's separation from God. You're alive physically, but your heart, your spirit, your soul, are dead toward God and you have no sense of fulfillment, no happiness, no real peace, no joy.

And then there's a third death, called the second death—eternal separation from God. Jesus called it outer darkness. He called it hell. Whatever it is, it's separation from God. We're all under the sentence of death. And what do we need most of all? Forgiveness.

Jesus became "the Lamb of God, who takes away the sin of the world!" (John 1:29)

We are guilty. We've broken God's moral law. God's moral law is expressed in the Ten Commandments and the Sermon on the Mount. The Bible says if we've broken even one of those commandments, we've broken them all (James 2:10). We're guilty, and because of that guilt, we are doomed to destruction and judgment. We're sinners who need the compassionate forgiveness of God.

That's why the Lord Jesus Christ took our death and our judgment and our hell on the cross. The Scriptures say, "God made him who had no sin to be sin for us" (2 Corinthians 5:21). Think of it, He had never committed adultery. He had never stolen anything. He had never lusted. He had never told a lie. He had never coveted anything, never committed a sin. Yet God took all the sins everyone has ever committed and laid them on Jesus. He became our substitute. He became "the Lamb of God, who takes away the sin of the world!" (John 1:29).

When Jesus said to the man with the palsy, "Be of good cheer; your sins are forgiven," He had all authority to do so. No other man, no other religious leader in the history of the world has ever said that. Who has that power but God?

Some of the people around Him didn't believe Him, so, in order to prove to them that He was God, he told the man, "Arise, take up your bed, and go to your house" (Matthew 9:6 NKJV). He not only forgave him his sins, but He healed his body, because Jesus Christ came for the whole person.

Don't Be Afraid of the Storms

The second time Jesus said "Be of good cheer" is found in Matthew 14:27: "Be of good cheer! It is I; do not be afraid" (NKJV). Jesus had just fed five thousand people with five loaves and two fishes (vv. 15–21) and then gone up to a mountain to pray (v. 23). The disciples got into a boat and went out on the sea. A storm came up. It was about to turn them over, and they were frightened. Just before sunrise, they saw what looked like a person walking on water. They couldn't believe it. They said, "It is a ghost!" (v. 26 NKJV).

And Jesus said, "Be of good cheer! It is I; do not be afraid."

One night I was on the west coast of Africa flying in a two-engine plane and had been talking to my seatmate, a British man, about God and the need to know Christ. He knew who I was, but he wasn't interested. All of a sudden, we hit a thunderstorm. People began to shout and scream. The man turned to me and said, "Dr. Graham, what were you saying?"

I'll be honest with you: I want to go to heaven, but I didn't want to go that night. I was terribly nervous myself, and I didn't try to hide it. But I began to talk to him about the Gospel again. He listened and asked some very intelligent questions, but when we got out of the storm and into the calm, he wasn't quite as interested.

I've had plenty of scary moments like that in my life. And so have you. In

Jesus is with you all day long. He's there in the most
ordinary things of life, and He's there in your troubles
and trials and bereavements and heartaches.

those moments, I've shot up a quick prayer to the Lord, and I've sensed a strange and wonderful peace come over me, "the peace of God, which transcends all understanding" (Philippians 4:7).

Let me tell you, Jesus is with you all day long. He's there in the most ordinary things of life, and He's there in your troubles and trials and bereavements and heartaches. When death comes to your family, He's there too.

Jesus Has Overcome the World

The third time Jesus said "be of good cheer" is found in John 16:33: "Be of good cheer, I have overcome the world" (NKJV). This was just before his prayer in the garden of Gethsemane. Jesus had the disciples in the upper room and was telling them all about how the world would hate them (15:19–20). He used the word *kosmos*, which means "world system of evil"—the evil that's in the world. There's much good in the world, but the dominant force in the world is evil. Jesus said, "This is the verdict: Light has come into the world, but people loved darkness instead of light because their deeds were evil. Everyone who does evil hates the light, and will not come into the light for fear that their deeds will be exposed" (3:19–20).

The disciples were getting discouraged. Jesus said, "They are going to take you out and scourge you if you follow Me" (Matthew 10:17, paraphrase). "They are going to persecute you. They may even kill you if you follow Me" (John 16:2, paraphrase). And that's the reason He said, "You must deny yourself and take up the cross if you're going to be My follower" (Matthew 16:24, paraphrase).

But then He said, "Be of good cheer, I have overcome the world." He assured them that "the one who is in you is greater than the one who is in the world" (1 John 4:4). When Jesus Christ died on the cross, the devil, who is the "prince of this world" (John 16:11), suffered a tremendous defeat. And when God raised Jesus from the dead, He showed the whole world that the devil and his forces are defeated.

You say, "If that's true, why do we have all the troubles we have? Why didn't God just kill the devil and get it all over with?" I've asked that question myself. But then I remember that everything is in the eternal present with God.

I remember an illustration I heard from a man in Los Angeles. "Do you remember in World War II, they had what they called D-Day, and that was the day that they invaded Normandy, France, under General Eisenhower? When they invaded that day, victory was assured over the Germans and the Nazis. But it took many months of fighting and dying and heartache and suffering and destruction until VE-Day (marking the Allied victory in Europe). We are now between D-Day and VE-Day. The victory has already been won at the cross and the resurrection. But the total victory will not come until the Lord Jesus Christ comes back again."

There's no problem too hard for God to solve.

Is there a problem that's too hard for you?

———————

Yes, God is greater than the world. Do you remember when God came to Abraham? Abraham was one hundred years old, and his wife was ninety-nine years old. God told Abraham to "look up at the sky and count the stars—if indeed you can count them." Then God said, "So shall your offspring be" (Genesis 15:5). When Sarah heard that, she laughed. She hadn't been able to have children. But then God said, "Is anything too hard for the LORD?" (Genesis 18:14). But God performed a miracle, and Abraham and Sarah had their child. There's no problem too hard for God to solve. Is there a problem that's too hard for you?

Let Not Your Heart Be Troubled

The last time Jesus told His disciples to be encouraged was when He said in John 14:1–3: "Let not your heart be troubled; you believe in God, believe also in Me. In My Father's house are many mansions; if it were not so, I would have told you. I go to prepare a place for you. And if I go and prepare a place for you, I will come again and receive you to Myself; that where I am, there you may be also" (NKJV).

There is an ultimate world coming where all problems will be solved. There'll be "no more death, nor sorrow, nor crying" (Revelation 21:4 NKJV). Just think—no goodbyes, no lack of money, no lack of food; just joy, happiness, and peace, forever and ever and ever. That world is on the way. We're told more than three hundred times in the New Testament that Jesus is coming back. And what a glorious hope we have that there will be "a new heaven and a new earth" (v. 1 NKJV). All things will be made new.

When Jesus ascended into heaven, the disciples stood there watching; they knew their Master was leaving them. Then two angels stood by them and said, "Men of Galilee, why do you stand gazing up into heaven? This same Jesus, who was taken up from you into heaven, will so come in like manner" (Acts 1:11 NKJV).

Yes, He's coming. The King is coming, the "King of kings and Lord of lords" (Revelation 19:16). Till then, we are to be faithful (Luke 12:42). As believers, we are to be the "salt of the earth" and the "light of the world" (Matthew 5:13–14).

There will be storms in life, but fear not. The end will come with the return of Jesus Christ. This is why a Christian can be an optimist. This is why a Christian can smile in the midst of the storms of life. Believe in the Lord Jesus Christ who is our refuge and strength. This is the victory that has overcome the world—faith in Him (1 John 5:4 NKJV).

Seven

GOD'S STRENGTH
IN WEAKNESS AND
COMFORT IN GRIEF

Blessed are those who mourn,

for they will be comforted.

MATTHEW 5:4

———

Grief turns us inward, but compassion turns us outward, and that's what we need when grief threatens to crush us. Whatever its cause, grief will come to all of us. We can experience comfort by giving comfort to others in their own perilous times because of what we've experienced ourselves.

Grief can kill a person emotionally and physically. If not counteracted with God's strength and power, our personal weakness may debilitate us. We can take refuge in our Savior and know for certain that we are not going through hardship alone. He may not take away trials, but He strengthens us through them. When we speak His name in prayer and cry out for His touch of compassion, perhaps He speaks our name to someone else who has been through disappointments and sorrow and brings kindred hearts together. The Bible says, "That their hearts might be comforted, being knit together in love" (Colossians 2:2 KJV).

Life can be like traveling a treacherous road. There are potholes that jolt us, detours that get us off course, and signs warning of danger ahead. The

The Bible's words are true: "There is a time for everything, and a season for every activity under the heavens: a time to be born and a time to die" (Ecclesiastes 3:1–2). This is a fact of life.

destination of soul and spirit is of utmost importance to God, so He offers us daily guidance. Some pay close attention to God's directions; others ignore them and speed past the flashing lights. No matter how we get there, everyone eventually arrives at the final destination: death's door. This is where the soul is separated from the body.

Grief is a reality; those who say we shouldn't grieve the loss of loved ones because they're "better off now" have not yet experienced the enormous hole that is left in our hearts when a loved one dies. Yes, if they're in heaven, they are better off—but we aren't better off. A major part of our lives has been ripped from us, and we grieve. Just as it takes time to heal from a major surgery, it also takes time to heal from the loss of someone we love. But for the Christian, we have certainty that life goes on in the presence of the Lord.

Paul's words to the believers in Thessalonica are true: "We . . . do not grieve like the rest of mankind, who have no hope" (1 Thessalonians 4:13). But we still grieve, and that is as it should be. Jesus wept as He stood by the tomb of His friend Lazarus, even though He knew that shortly He would bring Lazarus back to life (John 11:35).

You may not have been touched as yet by the death of anyone close to you, but grief comes to all at some point. The Bible's words are true: "There is a time for everything, and a season for every activity under the heavens: a time to be born and a time to die" (Ecclesiastes 3:1–2). This is a fact of life.

Coping with Grief

How should we cope with grief? Let me mention four steps that have helped me, not just as I have grieved my wife Ruth's death but as I have dealt with the deaths of my parents and in-laws, a brother and sister, and many relatives and friends over the years.

First, don't be surprised by your grief or deny it or feel guilty over it. Even when the death of someone we love is expected, we will still miss him or her, and we will still grieve our loss. Don't be surprised, either, if it creeps up on you at unexpected times and takes you by surprise.

Grieving is a process, and it doesn't go away overnight—even when we know our loved one's suffering has ended and they are now safely in heaven. When death comes to someone we love, we may feel numb at first (particularly if the death is unexpected); people may even comment on how well we are handling our grief. But then the numbness wears off, and the reality of what has happened may send us into periods of great sadness and unrelenting sorrow. People who have never experienced grief often can't understand this, but that should not make us think we are abnormal; nor should we deny our feelings and pretend everything is fine.

Second, don't focus only on the past, but also turn your heart and mind to the future. I have found this a helpful exercise in times of grief. When someone close to us dies, we naturally focus on what that person meant to us in the past. We remember the good times we had and how our love bound us together even in hard times. We sense, too, the crushing finality of death and realize as never before that the past is gone forever, and it will never be repeated. It's not wrong to do this; in fact, it is perfectly natural.

But as time passes, we will need to turn our thoughts to the future. That isn't easy to do; we don't want to face the pain and emptiness we know we are going to feel in the months and years ahead. It's easier to focus on the memories of the past. But we still have people who love us and need us, and we still have responsibilities. Most of all, God is not finished with us; He still has a plan for the remainder of our lives. Paul's words concerning his own spiritual journey apply to us even when we grieve: "One thing I do: Forgetting what is behind and straining toward what is ahead, I press on toward the goal to win the prize for which God has called me heavenward in Christ Jesus" (Philippians 3:13–14).

Sometimes, however, the future intrudes on us in ways we would rather avoid. No one wants to face the legal and financial issues that must be settled shortly after someone's death; no one wants to face the task of cleaning out a spouse's closet or desk. But don't be forced into making hasty decisions that you may later regret.

Forcing our hearts and minds to look toward the future means accepting

All around you are people who have burdens, and God can use your experience to encourage and help them.

what has happened and—little by little—learning to live with it. It also means that we begin resuming our normal activities and contacts—not necessarily all at once but, nevertheless, resisting the temptation to remain withdrawn. It may take a deliberate act of the will on our part to restart our normal routines, but it is important to do so.

Third, begin reaching out to others who need your help. I have never met a person who wasn't weighed down by some kind of problem or burden. God wants to help carry those burdens. One way He does that is by sending someone into the person's life who can share the burden. Grief is a heavy burden, and we need to be willing to let others reach out and help us carry it instead of our trying to shoulder it all alone. And in the process, we can share their burdens too.

Paul reminds us to "carry each other's burdens, and in this way you will fulfill the law of Christ" (Galatians 6:2). He tells us also to "rejoice with those who rejoice; mourn with those who mourn" (Romans 12:15). All around you are people who have burdens, and God can use your experience to encourage and help them.

There are those in your church or neighborhood carrying a burden of grief right now. Ask God to help you be a friend to them. More than most people, you can understand what they are going through, and you can help relieve the weight of their burden by your concern. Sometimes all they need is someone who will listen. Remember that God is "the Father of compassion and the God of all comfort, who comforts us in all our troubles, so that we can comfort those in any trouble with the comfort we ourselves receive from God" (2 Corinthians 1:3–4).

When we reach out to others, we help not only them but ourselves as well because we are distracted from our own grief.

Fourth, and most importantly, take your burden of grief to God. God knows what you are going through, and He loves you and wants to help you. Remember that He knows what it is to grieve because He watched as His only Son was put to death. Jesus was "a Man of sorrows and acquainted with grief" (Isaiah 53:3 NKJV). In His great love for us, Jesus promised to send the Holy Spirit to comfort us in our time of need.

God Meets Us in Our Grief

How does God help us cope with grief? First, He assures us of His presence. We are never alone if we know Christ; He lives within us by His Spirit. Even when you don't feel His presence, it doesn't change the fact that He is with you every moment of the day. God's promise is for you: "Do not fear, for I am with you; do not be dismayed, for I am your God. I will strengthen you and help you; I will uphold you with my righteous right hand" (Isaiah 41:10).

In the midst of your grief, turn daily to God's Word, and let its promises

In the midst of your grief, turn daily to God's Word,
and let its promises encourage and sustain you.

encourage and sustain you. Remember to "cast your cares on the LORD and he will sustain you; he will never let the righteous be shaken" (Psalm 55:22).

Then God also helps us by assuring us of His goodness. When we lose a loved one, usually all we can think about is our own grief and how empty we feel. Instead we should remember God's blessings and have a spirit of gratitude—gratitude for the life of our loved one, gratitude for all he or she meant to us, and most of all, gratitude that death ushers a saved soul into God's presence forever. A daily "attitude of gratitude" will do much to move us beyond our sorrow.

Comfort the Grieving

You may not be dealing with the death of a loved one right now; you might even feel it's a bit morbid to give much thought to it—until it happens to you. But even if you aren't touched personally by grief for some time to come, others around you will be—friends, coworkers, relatives, even casual acquaintances.

Caring takes many forms—from running errands for a family who has lost a loved one to making yourself available by lending a listening ear to someone going through a crisis. There are countless opportunities to comfort others in hard times. Remember, God doesn't comfort us to make us comfortable but to make us comforters. It also opens a door to share the hope we have in Christ.

Turning Toward God and Others in Our Grief

When tragedy or suffering strikes, we have a decision to make. Will we turn away from God, or will we turn toward Him? Which road will we take? One road leads to doubt, anger, bitterness, fear, hopelessness, and despair. The other leads to hope, comfort, peace, strength, and joy. No one welcomes pain, emptiness, loneliness, and death—but God has not abandoned us. Even in the midst of life's greatest sorrows, His Word is still true: "Never will I leave you; never will I forsake you" (Hebrews 13:5).

We may find that our own loads grow lighter when we begin helping others. Our choices determine our destiny. When we make choices with the Lord Jesus at the center, life's journey can be purposeful and filled with hope that one day we will be reunited with all those who have impacted our lives.

We should be about our Father's business by pouring His compassionate love into aching and parched souls who have nowhere to turn, no one to love, and no one to care. Let them see Jesus in us—in the good times and the bad. That is a living testimony.

Eight

GOD STRENGTHENS OUR
FAITH, HOPE, AND LOVE

And now these three remain:

faith, hope and love. But the

greatest of these is love.

1 CORINTHIANS 13:13

———

Faith points us beyond our problems to the hope we have in Christ; it is He who demonstrates the immeasurable love of God by bringing us to salvation. Do you want your faith to grow in Christ? Do you long for hope? Do you desire God's love to fill you? Then let the Bible saturate your mind and soul.

Your faith may be just a little thread. It may be small and weak, but act on that faith. It does not matter how big your faith is but, rather, where your faith is. By faith in Jesus we can be forgiven of our sins and have hope in God's eternal love.

But when doubt reigns, faith cannot abide. When despair lingers, hope is crushed. Where hatred rules, love is crowded out.

Christians who are strong in the faith grow as they accept whatever God allows to enter their lives. Faith, hope, and love are pillars that we build upon in good times and especially difficult times. Faith comes by hearing, and hearing by the word of God (Romans 10:17). Hope strengthens us (Isaiah 40:31). And God's love is what compels us to obey Him (1 John 5:2).

Faith, hope, and love are pillars
that we build upon in good times
and especially difficult times.

The whole world is looking for hope. It seems that both on the home front and in our world, hopelessness pervades. In fact, those who are without God have no hope.

Paul said it this way in Ephesians 2:12: "At that time you were separate from Christ . . . without hope and without God in the world." The Bible tells us that there's a glorious future ahead when Jesus Christ comes back again, but you don't have that hope if you don't have Christ in your heart.

Love is the greatest of these and is the very thing that every Christian should be filled with and exemplify. We ought to have love written on our faces and in our hearts—toward everybody. But for many, despair and hopelessness prevail. Why?

Looking for an Escape

Our culture will stand in roaring ovations for the illusionists, escape artists, and magicians. Deception is everything opposite of the truth. Escapism is everywhere these days. It's ironic that in our frenzied attempts to achieve happiness, we are finding everything *but* happiness. So we look for ways to escape the disappointments of life.

There's the *escape of imagination*. Scripture says in Romans 1:21, "Their thinking became futile and their foolish hearts were darkened." What do you imagine while you enjoy leisure time or when you're lying in bed at night? What do you dream or think about? The Bible says Satan, the devil, is an "angel of light" (2 Corinthians 11:14). He does a good job of selling the unreal.

There's the *escape of pleasure*: escape into passion, appetite, desire, sex fantasy. Some escape into drugs and alcohol. But these things don't give peace or joy or satisfaction. They don't fill the void in our hearts.

Thousands of people, old and young, are looking to fill that void, even those who think they know Christ. Too many, however, have never really given their lives to Christ. They've never invited Him in. They joined a church and were baptized and confirmed. But deep in their hearts, they've not experienced that personal relationship with Christ that they could have every minute of the day.

We are a people who need constant mental stimulation. We get up in the morning, and the first thing we do is turn on the TV. We get in our cars and turn on the radio, or we talk on our cell phones as we walk down the street. We surf the internet or play mindless games on our phones.

In Mark 8, Jesus told His disciples they should be following Him with their whole hearts. Then He asked, "What good is it for someone to gain the whole world, yet forfeit their soul?" That soul that lives inside of your body is going to live forever. Taking care of that is far more important than anything else.

Jesus Christ will love you back
for the rest of your life with
a love that is deeper than any
human love you'll ever know.

Reader's Digest once said that, in order to be happy, a person must have some-one to love, something to do, and something to hope for. Jesus Christ is that someone to love. He will love you back for the rest of your life with a love that is deeper than any human love you'll ever know. This is His promise, and any hope we have is based in that promise.

The Hope of Righteousness

So what hope does Jesus offer? First, there's the *hope of righteousness*. Galatians 5:5 says, "For through the Spirit we eagerly await by faith the righteousness for which we hope." You have to have righteousness before you can come into the kingdom of God—but we don't have it. So where do we find it? You don't have it. I don't have it. I've never been righteous in my life; I've never been sinless. I'm a sinner. And the Bible says that sinners are lost and doomed and are going to face the judgment and hell.

Where do we get this righteousness? Christ purchased it for us at the cross. And when you come to the cross, He clothes you in His righteousness so that when you come before God, He doesn't see *you*; He sees the righteousness of Christ instead of you, and He accepts you and receives you because of that.

When we regard religion as law, we then live in terror; but the grace of God gives us confidence.

The Hope of Salvation

There's the *hope of salvation* too. "Believe in the Lord Jesus, and you will be saved" (Acts 16:31). Has that happened to you? *Believe* is the key word. Put your confidence in nothing but Christ. That means you'll have to give up some things that are wrong in your life because when you come to repentance, you have to say, "Lord, I'm sorry for the things that I've done wrong. I'm willing to turn from them and give them up if You'll help me now."

The Bible says, "Salvation is found in no one else, for there is no other name under heaven given to mankind by which we must be saved" (Acts 4:12). In 2 Corinthians 1:10 it says, "He has delivered us from such a deadly peril, and he will deliver us again. On him we have set our hope that he will continue to deliver us." This carries with it the idea that God delivers us from a great deal of the misery and psychological problems and spiritual problems in this world. Many times He delivers us from physical perils as well.

Many of us have heard and known of Corrie ten Boom, who went through the Nazi death camps at Ravensbrück. Her sister died in the camp, but when Corrie was released, she said, "The best is yet to come!" And she continued to say that for the rest of her life.

The best for us is yet to come if we're in Christ. There's nothing hopeless about our future. There's nothing but joy, gladness, encouragement, and excitement as we look to the future.

The Hope of Eternal Life

There's also the *hope of eternal life*. People seem to be more fascinated today about life after death than any time I can remember.

Dostoyevsky, the great Russian writer, in his book *The Brothers Karamazov*, wrote, "If you were to destroy in mankind the belief of immortality"—you didn't believe in heaven—"not only love but every living force maintaining the life of the world would at once be dried up."

In Titus 1:2, the Scripture ensures those who believe "the hope of eternal life, which God, who does not lie, promised before the beginning of time." Think of it—before the world ever began, God promised life in heaven to all those who put their faith and trust in His Son, Jesus Christ.

The word *eternal* doesn't mean that you just live on and on and on and on.

The best for us is yet to come if we're in Christ. There's nothing but joy, gladness, encouragement, and excitement as we look to the future.

That's only part of it. It also implies quality of life. You'll have a high quality of life the rest of eternity, but you'll also have a much higher quality of life here and now till that moment comes when you meet God.

Then there's the *hope of the coming again of Jesus Christ*. Believers are to be "looking for the blessed hope and glorious appearing of our great God and Savior Jesus Christ" (Titus 2:13 NKJV). That's my hope. I am looking for His coming back to this earth any time. I wake up some mornings and say, "Lord, is this the day You're going to come and take us to heaven?"

The New Testament is full of hope and expectancy: "Our [hope] is in heaven; from which we also eagerly wait for the Savior, the Lord Jesus Christ" (Philippians 3:20 NKJV). I'm looking for Him. The Bible says that someday He's going to break open the heavens, and you'll see the angels, the armies of heaven. Then He will make this a clean world. It'll be a world of joy and happiness and fulfillment where you'll know your loved ones and friends. Most important, though, is that you will see Christ.

That promise will someday become literal history, and with God's help, we're going to be a part of that history that is yet to come. "There were loud voices in heaven, which said: 'The kingdom of the world has become the kingdom of our Lord and of his Messiah, and he will reign for ever and ever'" (Revelation 11:15).

Man will never achieve the kingdom of God on earth. Only Jesus Christ, when He comes back, will be able to bring it. He will defeat every enemy. Sin will be eliminated. Death will be eliminated. War will be eliminated. Crime will be eliminated. It'll be personal redemption. And you yourself will be there if you know Christ.

The hope of the second coming of Christ generates energy and sacrifice and faithfulness and diligence and zeal. It makes me excited to even think about it. Martin Luther said, "I live as though Christ died yesterday, rose again today, and is coming tomorrow."

Tens of thousands of God's saints through the ages have found their dark nights lightened and tortured souls strengthened because they found help from God's Spirit in the Word of God. When brothers and sisters in Christ unite in the common bond of Scripture and prayer, they are strengthened in their faith and witness, for we are stewards of the Gospel message—and are given the power to proclaim the greatest news in heaven and earth.

Nine

GOD STRENGTHENS OUR
PURPOSE AND CALLING

How, then, can they call on the one they have not believed in? And how can they believe in the one of whom they have not heard? And how can they hear without someone preaching to them? And how can anyone preach unless they are sent?

Romans 10:14–15

Every Christian should become an ambassador of Christ. Every Christian should be so filled with holy fervor that nothing could ever quench his or her passion. Oh, that we would capture some of the magnificent obsession that the early Christians had.

The famous novelist Lloyd Douglas coined the phrase "magnificent obsession." The early apostles had a magnificent obsession to turn the world upside down with their message. When Paul and Silas were ministering in Thessalonica, they were accused of this: "These who have turned the world upside down have come here too" (Acts 17:6 NKJV). The people of Jesus' day accused Him of being "beside Himself" (Mark 3:21 KJV). Governor Festus said to the apostle Paul after listening to him speak, "You are out of your mind, Paul! . . . Your great learning is driving you insane" (Acts 26:24). But Paul had an obsession.

When men and women offer to go to the hard places of the world to serve Christ, they, too, are often accused of being out of their minds. The apostle Paul

These men and women of the past have handed us a torch. We, too, must have their obsession. And we must dare to believe God for even greater things.

said, "If we are 'out of our mind,' as some say, it is for God; if we are in our right mind, it is for you. For Christ's love compels us" (2 Corinthians 5:13–14).

Think of the glorious daring of those early apostles. Little wonder that the world called them mad. Paul was satisfied with nothing less than taking the Gospel to the whole world, including imperial Rome. Magnificent obsessions indeed, every one of them. Who could understand their zeal?

They carried the flaming truths of the Gospel far and wide. They surmounted obstacles and overcame difficulties and endured persecution. And that was their answer to Christ's command: the magnificent obsession of obeying Christ.

These men and women of the past have handed us a torch. We, too, must have their obsession. And we must dare to believe God for even greater things.

The social needs of the world are tremendous. Social injustice is everywhere. But the spiritual needs are there, too, and there's no dichotomy. The whole human race is suffering from the spiritual disease of sin, and only Christ and His Gospel can meet it.

It's my prayer that a "magnificent obsession"—the love of God in Christ—will so constrain you that you will offer to serve His cause. To surrender yourself to the lordship of Christ. To use your gifts for His service. Every believer is called to be a testimony for Him.

Itinerant evangelists are the most important ambassadors and messengers on earth. They are a mighty army, spreading out across the world with a vision to reach their own people for Christ. You and I, God's ambassadors, are called to sound the warning, to call sinners to repentance, to point the way to peace with God and the hope that is in Christ. Let's represent Christ with a fervor that will put all worldly enthusiasm to shame.

Representing Christ

There are four things I want you to consider as you think about how you will represent Christ.

First, consider the command we received from the Lord Jesus Christ. Just before His ascension, Jesus said, "You will receive power when the Holy Spirit comes on you; and you will be my witnesses in Jerusalem, and in all Judea and Samaria, and to the ends of the earth" (Acts 1:8).

Notice what Jesus said all through the Gospels: "Go and do." "Go and show." "Go out quickly into the streets and into the lanes." "Go out into the highways and hedges." "Go to the vineyard." "Go into the village." "Go into the city." "Go into the towns." "Go to the lost sheep." "Go and preach the kingdom of God." "Go into all the world." Jesus frequently used these two verbs: *come* and *go*. Isn't it interesting that the "Gospel" begins with the word *Go*?

Then Jesus calls out to the world, "Come to me, all you who are weary and burdened, and I will give you rest" (Matthew 11:28). "Come to the cross for salvation," He calls. "Come be reconciled to God." "Come repent of your sins." And then, when we have, He says, "Go into the world and be a witness in the world, even unto death."

With His commands ringing in their ears, the disciples set out not only to reach the world but to turn it upside down. They suffered hardship and persecution and floggings and beatings and death, but they said, "We cannot help speaking about what we have seen and heard" (Acts 4:20). They were a people under authority. They went because they'd been sent.

If ever there was a time that the world needed to be turned upside down, it's now. Will we go and be witnesses for Him?

Second, consider the message we proclaim. Time after time in church history, the message has been blunted, watered down, diluted . . . it has lost its power. The early apostles had no doubt about their message. They said, "Salvation is found in no one else" (Acts 4:12). They knew there was no other way for a person to be saved except through the Lord Jesus Christ.

God has a great message, and He wants us to deliver it to the world. A message of hope. Yes, we're sinners, but God says, "I love you! I sent My Son to die on the cross for you. I raised Him from the dead. He's coming back. He's the future world ruler. I will give you eternal life."

That's good news to a despairing world. And He's asked you to be His ambassador.

Third, consider the people we're to reach. Jesus said, "to all nations, beginning at Jerusalem" (Luke 24:47). Your "Jerusalem" is where you live—your school, your workplace, your home, your family, your friends.

The world that our Lord is talking about includes the geographical world, but it also includes the psychological and the sociological world. It includes the world of school and business and government and labor. I challenge you to be a witness for Christ wherever God sends you.

The doors are more open today than they've ever been. They're open to you, with the Gospel, because the world is searching and grasping desperately for an answer.

The fields are "ripe for harvest" (John 4:35). But I warn you that harvest time is brief. Jesus said, "Night is coming, when no one can work" (John 9:4). Go now. Do now. Prepare now to proclaim the Gospel. The Gospel is urgent, and the lost are dying in need of the Savior.

Fourth, consider the power that Christ imparts to us. There are twenty-three Hebrew and Greek words in the Bible translated "power." The one that Jesus used is the one I want to mention: "You will receive power when the Holy Spirit comes on you" (Acts 1:8).

Years ago, there was a photograph in *Life* magazine that showed a straw that

I challenge you to be a witness for
Christ wherever God sends you.

had penetrated a light pole during a tornado. I asked myself how such a fragile straw could penetrate a light pole. It was because the power of the wind that was driving it was so tremendous. Christ has promised a power far greater than that. Our power comes from the Holy Spirit. You're not going to your Jerusalem or to the uttermost part of the world without God's power.

The Spirit prepares hearts. The Spirit guides us. The Spirit gives us boldness. The Spirit has given us the Word of God. The Spirit gives us wisdom. The Spirit alone can bring conviction and faith. Therefore, we are dependent on Him.

Saying Yes to Your Calling

In the latter part of the nineteenth century, there was a wealthy, highly educated athlete at Cambridge University who was probably one of the greatest cricket players of his day. His name was C. T. Studd. In a great spiritual awakening at Cambridge, Studd was converted. He resigned from the celebrated "Cambridge Eleven" cricket team and instead led the "Cambridge Seven" as frontier missionaries—a movement that triggered one of the most momentous movements of modern missions. Reflecting on what made him do it, Studd said this: "If Jesus Christ be God and died for me, no sacrifice can be too great for me to make for Him."

Adoniram Judson was born in a Congregational minister's home. By the time he was five, his father was already teaching him to read Greek. As a young man, Judson went to Brown University. The university was filled with unbelief and agnosticism and skepticism. His roommate was named Ernest, and they went through college together as unbelievers. When they graduated, neither was a Christian.

Judson was riding horseback through New England when he stopped one night at an inn and asked for a room. The innkeeper said, "There's only one room left, and it's next door to a man who is dying. He's making an awful racket; I don't think you'll be able to sleep." Judson said, "It doesn't make any difference to me; give me the room." So they put up his horse, and he went up to the room. Nighttime came, and he heard a voice in the next room. Sometimes it asked God for mercy, and sometimes it swore and took the name of God in vain. At some point in the night, the voice stopped, and Judson fell asleep.

The next morning he asked the innkeeper, "What happened to the man in the room next to me last night?" The innkeeper said, "He died." And Judson asked, "What was his name?" The innkeeper told him the man's name was Ernest—and it was the same Ernest who had been Judson's roommate throughout college. Judson got on his horse, and every time the horse's hooves hit the ground, the words kept running through his mind: "Dead." "Lost." "Dead." "Lost." "Dead." "Lost." "Dead." "Lost." He turned around and went home.

God is not calling us tonight to a playground or a sports arena; He's calling us to a battleground. God has promised us His full resources in the battle.

He entered Andover Theological Seminary, and there he was converted and came to know Christ as his Savior. As a result of that conversion, he got a vision for the world and became the first missionary to leave American shores for the foreign field. He went to India and then on to Burma. Today, thousands of Christians in Southeast Asia call him blessed.

God's Great Calling for You

God is calling us. We can respond, "Yes, Lord, I will go where You want me to go. I'll be what You want me to be," or we can say, "No, Lord, I'm not going to surrender that much to You. I'll give You 50 percent, 75 percent, maybe 80 percent, but I can't go all the way. The price is too high."

"For whoever wants to save their life will lose it, but whoever loses their life for me will find it" (Matthew 16:25). God is not calling us tonight to a playground or a sports arena; He's calling us to a battleground. God has promised us His full resources in the battle.

The story is told of the famous organ at Freiburg Cathedral in Germany. The man who'd played it for many years had become very old. One day a stranger came in and asked if he could play the organ. The old man said, "No. I'm the only one allowed to play this organ." The stranger persisted. Finally the old man gave in. The stranger began to play beautiful music like nothing the old organist had ever heard. His eyes began to fill with tears, and when the stranger finished playing, the old man asked, "What is your name?" The answer came back, "My name is Felix Mendelssohn." The old man told the story over and over again. And he would always end by shaking his head and saying, "To think I almost did not allow the world's greatest master to play on this organ."

Jesus Christ has spoken to you. You could be on the verge of missing God's great call on your life. If you answer yes, you're in obedience to Him, and that brings fulfillment, joy, and peace in this life and rewards in the life to come. But if you say no—which is your privilege and right—it means you'll continue to wander, and the questions will be harder. And the answers will be more difficult.

God wants you to live life to the fullest. He offers you the assurance that your sin is forgiven and that you're going to heaven. He has a plan for you that will prosper you and bless you and, indeed, take you to heaven when you die. God wants you to live, but the choice is yours.

When you say, "Lord, I'm weak and I'm a sinner. I need help, and I'm putting out my hand to You. Will You take it?" Then He'll do it, and He'll give you strength to overcome the temptations that come to us all.

We may long to be rescued out of despair, but God may want to strengthen us in the midst of it. Just think: Had Jesus been rescued from the cross by His Father, the ransom for sin would have never been paid. For this profound reason, God sent Jesus on a rescue mission to save the souls of mankind, and Jesus was obedient to the Father's calling when He said, "Not my will, but thine" (Luke 22:42 KJV).

Can we humble ourselves before the Lord in obedience and truly give ourselves in service to Him? To know the will of God is the highest of all wisdom. Living in the center of God's will rules out all falseness of religion and puts the stamp of true sincerity upon our service to God. The greatest testimony to this dark world would be a band of crucified and risen men and women, dead to sin and alive unto God, bearing in their bodies "the marks of the Lord Jesus" (Galatians 6:17 NKJV).

LIFE IS HARD, BUT
HEAVEN IS GLORIOUS

We know that if the earthly

tent we live in is destroyed,

we have a building from God,

an eternal house in heaven,

not built by human hands.

2 CORINTHIANS 5:1

———

The journey God has set before us isn't a freeway; we are constantly encountering forks and junctions, crossroads and detours. Which way will we go when we meet them? Life can be hard; it is filled with decisions, and we can't avoid them. For centuries mankind has been on this incredible journey, taking him across every generation and through every conceivable experience in his search for God. We mustn't let the burdens and hardships of this life distract us. We must keep our eyes firmly fixed on what God has promised at the end of our journey—heaven itself!

I don't believe I have ever known a person (or at least a Christian) who did not want to know what heaven is like—including me! This is not mere curiosity, however. It's not like wondering about some place we've never visited. As Christians, we know that heaven is our final home—the place where we will be spending all eternity. Why wouldn't we want to know what heaven will be like?

The Glory of Heaven

We sometimes speak of a beautiful sunset or a warm spring day as "glorious," but even earth's most awe-inspiring nature is but a shadow of the glory of heaven.

Why is heaven glorious? For one supreme reason: it is the dwelling place of God. Think of it—if you know Jesus Christ, someday you will be safely in His presence forever! I can barely imagine what that will be like—but it will be glorious beyond description. Not only is heaven glorious, but it is also perfect. This shouldn't surprise us: since God is perfect, so, too, is heaven, His dwelling place.

Think of all the sins and evils that now afflict us: disease, death, loneliness, fear, sorrow, temptation, disappointment, disability, addiction, war, conflict, anger, jealousy, greed—the list is almost endless. But in heaven, all those will be banished! "He will wipe every tear from their eyes. There will be no more death or mourning or crying or pain, for the old order of things has passed away. . . . Nothing impure will ever enter it" (Revelation 21:4, 27).

In heaven we will be perfect. More than that, in God's time we will be given new bodies—free from all the limitations and frailties of our present bodies.

Not only will heaven be glorious and perfect, but it will also be joyous. How could it be anything less? Its glory, its perfection—these alone would be enough to bring us unimaginable joy. But heaven will be joyous also because that's where all our questions will be answered. Someday all our doubts and questions will be resolved, and we will understand. Heaven will be joyous because all our burdens will be lifted—never to return.

The Place Called Forever

The Bible tells us one final truth about heaven's joy: our experience of heaven will express itself in joyous worship. On this earth, our worship is imperfect, incomplete, superficial—even dull or boring. But in heaven, our worship will be perfect because we will see our Savior face-to-face.

When life's burdens press upon you, or its pressures seem more than you can bear, turn your heart toward your heavenly home: "Even though I walk through the darkest valley, I will fear no evil, for you are with me; your rod and your staff, they comfort me. . . . Surely your goodness and love will follow me all the days of my life, and I will dwell in the house of the Lord forever" (Psalm 23:4, 6). When your hopes and dreams fall apart or when people disappoint you or turn against you, turn your heart toward your heavenly home. And when infirmities and struggles threaten to overwhelm you, turn your heart toward your heavenly home.

The moment we take our last breath on earth, we take our first in heaven. This most wonderful place, and its benefits for believers, are out of this world!

BILLY GRAHAM EVANGELISTIC ASSOCIATION

P. O. Box 1270
Charlotte, NC 28201-1270

BGEA Website
billygraham.org

BGEA phone number
1-877-247-2426

BGEA Prayer Line
1-855-255-PRAY (7729)

Billy Graham Library website
billygrahamlibrary.org

Billy Graham Archive and Research Center website
billygrahamarchivecenter.com

Billy Graham Training Center at The Cove website
thecove.org

ABOUT THE AUTHOR

Billy Graham (1918–2018), world-renowned preacher, evangelist, and author, delivered the Gospel message to more people face-to-face than anyone in history and ministered on every continent of the world in almost 200 countries and territories. His ministry extended far beyond stadiums and arenas, utilizing radio, television, film, print media, wireless communications, and thirty-three books, all that still carry the Good News of God's redemptive love for mankind. Engraved on a simple fieldstone in the Memorial Prayer Garden where he is buried at the Billy Graham Library in Charlotte, North Carolina, these words exemplify how the man and the minister wished to be remembered: "Preacher of the Gospel of the Lord Jesus Christ."

GOD IS WITH YOU ALL THE TIME

When the world around you feels chaotic and hard to navigate, you can be reminded of the unchanging truths of the Bible in these 365-day devotionals from beloved evangelist Billy Graham.

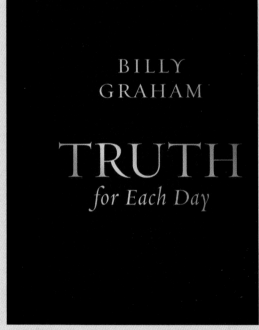

BILLY GRAHAM

TRUTH
for Each Day

Truth for Each Day
ISBN: 978-1-4002-4436-2

BILLY
GRAHAM

PEACE
for Each Day

BILLY
GRAHAM

WISDOM
for Each Day

Peace for Each Day	Wisdom for Each Day
ISBN: 978-1-4002-2411-1	ISBN: 978-1-4002-1123-4

Experience it for yourself.

The BILLY GRAHAM Library

FREE ADMISSION

Bring your friends and family to see a powerful story of hope unfold at the Billy Graham Library. Together, you can explore engaging multimedia presentations, displays, photos, and memorabilia. Come discover how God used a dairy farmer's son to tell the world about His love—and see for yourself how this never-changing message changes everything.